The Port
of Los Angeles

Jane Sprague

chax 2009

ISBN 978 0 925904 77 5

Acknowledgments

Portions of this manuscript have been previously published in the journals *Primary Writing* (5/06); *Tarpaulin Sky* (Summer, 2005); *Xcp: Streetnotes* (Fall, 2004); *Foursquare* (Vol. 1 No. 6) and as the chapbooks *The Port of Los Angeles* (Subpoetics, 2004); *fuck your pastoral* (Subpoetics, 2005) and *Entropic Liberties* (with Jonathan Skinner; Dusie, 2006).

CONTENTS

THE PORT OF LOS ANGELES

Goods on a truck mid-country awaited transport
to their new destination abode domicile
their new place of domestic malcontent

the goods waited in their precious and stained ways
their ways of chipped edges and past fights
their held litanies of the sounds of sex
held sounds cries to sleep after raging

held memories of the things they'd contained
things smoked and inhaled
held memories of naming and also the names
spoken secrets only the objects heard

because they held these things and waited
small ships in tight bays

because their way of portage was defined as a way of cigarettes smoking to cinder
to ash over the wheel
a way of ash between the driver's legs

the crease in the jeans
the smell of the companion
too close in the adjacent seat

the goods awaited swift transport through many states and witnessed
many things

cities smog animals
passing through slaughter passing through ways of metal cages metal cars
metal blades passing into cool foam snapped plastic passing into cold
reefer cars

the goods saw this and waited patiently
a word beyond patience
a word beyond the spark of perfectly timed fireworks
in the Arch strapped country under the light of a just full moon

the things saw this and held the memory of what they were into
what destination hence and with whom
what nation to pass through and study
what new port to arrive
what vessel what container
what soft hand to greet them

same hand
same sound
same nation city street
same point of departure
as point of arrival

cranes of the port
the longshoreworkers
the heroin creeping in jackets
the hundreds of plastic things shaped for fixing mending catching all manner
of debris

because the things knew this and slept

because the things knew of a use beyond the sound of their names

they waited

not idle

not indifferent

parsed into sectors or boxes of labeled and specific function or rooms of
disbursement

they waited

and waited

to arrive.

flowers of **The Commons**: petunia
boxes: a cruder tool to keep the
common people out

**are you as common as a napkin a needle a knife?
or are you a very fine well aged wine?**

the cultural studies section of the long beach barnes and
noble consists of about eleven shelves. or one hefty book
case. only, you aren[...]ets.
books about being g[...]ver-
sion of cultural stud[...] de-
pendent bookstores [...] in
ithaca there is a hu[...] the
barnes and noble. i[...]ble
it is a slim shelf. but[...] and
adore barthes.

am reading derrida. [...]uld
just bite it and go f[...] e a
focus here. help me g[...]

along the lines of wh[...]uld
like reading guillerm[...]ey
are not poets. they a[...] the
bodies that were not[...]ge.
would like to re-rea[...]n a
truck somewhere wo[...]

in a small place a town place
GOWN GIRDLE CAP & TASSLE
one person sat in a rocker on a porch
in a small place a made place high on a
HILL HILLOCK TURRET TOWER
porch in a rocker under sky one drew a
map of this place that section
where put
where rank
room at the table
one spoke
IT IS OF MULTIPLE AUDIENCES
IT IS OF DIFFIDENT CLASS
IT IS OF VALUE ADDED NOTIONS
the listening party disagreed.
site specific noun of institutional affiliation: HERE
the listening party decided to remove
herself from [not only the equation] but
also the place
Jean-Luc Nancy Pierre Bourdieu Jean-Jacques Rousseau
Raymond Williams
skin ivory palm kidskin word silent
touch push hand of cover mouth
at the end
fine fine affable gait
walk walk
                                                away

which is why more s[...] to
irvine. or see if ucla will have back.

want to ask you things. but you are not talking to me.
dont know why. maybe am speaking directly into the
blocked senders vault. dear blocked senders vault
please tell am doing that thinking about class urged
me to do. tell never mixed up with the monolith with
the institution please tell it is different to be would you
also tell that there is a way of excellence and strength
in insisting on community work and the questioning
of the community would you tell that community it-
self is ephemeral at best and yes, do understand that.

we have arrived

the big empty

we follow yachts

the path of canals

we watch fires burn

Courtney Love tied down and thrashing

Michael Jackson's felt codpiece

this is the nightly news

this is the promised land

when we arrive

Kobe stays

Shaquille sells himself away

the Lakers still godly

in San Onofre

great whites lured by last year's buried whale

bump surfers

we purchase as little as possible

watch the hammer derricks drill

hoping for oil

hoping and hoping for oil

we find comfort in thrift

reheat yesterday's coffee

buy generic brands only

California insinuates itself through our veins through our beds

through our children through the constant hump and suck of the

waves

as the derricks continue to drill

we find ourselves called to Ikea again and again

strange comfort Scandinavian curves

our child falls in love with Ikea and wants to move in

our child finds comfort small beds small nesting places

we wonder bunks of the port small spaces for ships small pockets

for junk

we arrive in familiar utterly strange

inhale smoke float into silence

inhale smoke consider lines on the face of our friends

we consider love and fucking

we pine.

we follow helicopter beams to the beach

we watch the bust from afar

watch sirens flare flickerblue

watch people handcuffed wade through water to beach to car to confinement

we watch the one who gets away

people locked in containers

people locked in and let out

the junk

goods for Ikea

the women

the men

the junk

animals in pockets and containers

workers

ways of work

ways of sleep

placeless

our narrow beds full of sweat the dream our lover is dreaming in

the far adjacent state

we pine for sleep and our lovers

we think these things alone and concurrently as the derricks

continue to drill their hopeful tap tapping waiting for oil

waiting for our arrival our bunk our bed our slumber to cease or

begin

still the derricks are moving

drills in the night moving

through our arrival

ushering us past

back to the place of our goods carried and sold

our goods handled and packed

our goods broken in anger and drunkenness

our goods secret notes sealed tightly with gum

still we are riddled with this sense of waiting

to arrive

to be filled

to get there somehow

to come

to get off

to own

or release

to hit the silky vein

the promise

as if the liquid of that would be enough

as if the junk could smoke us far enough into stillness

far enough into some cool made nest

as if that promise of safety could wrap us

as our legs wrap us in the night

one to the each to the other to the imagined

to the next to the palm between the thigh

as if the absence of that thing is place enough and there enough

and good

in shipping lanes and sheets

our shared oily skin shared oily sheets

shared lanes of oil lanes of derricks drilling unceasingly

a rhythm for sleep

a new dream

super containers

extreme engineering

extreme global village

as much as we were trying to live simply
as much as we tried to discard our possessions
we became more and more part of the problem

as we moved further and further from our small eden
our perfect worm compost our lovely dirt roads
our imperfect idyll

with its perfect unemployment its perfect racism
its perfect exclusion of that perfectly pitched and heldback class
as we watched our child step deeper and deeper into the mind of his peers
our nation's rural poor

as we watched this and despaired
as we watched this and despaired for the rent
as we got a better job and gave everything away

the myth of California was the same

and John Steinbeck was right

but the world was bigger now

and we did not want to be here

still the wind was warm

the food was good at Ikea

the goods were durable
cheap
and well fashioned

we found ourselves perfectly pitched at the edge of globalism

the lip

it seemed like a word too big and better suited for the news

or at least CNN

we were transfixed by the ships rolling in

we worried

we were vexed

nettled

beset

were we merely imitating at best

were we making cheap concessions for our impending descent into the

mass bourgeoisie

consumers being consumed

was there any way to escape it

was asking this question too much in light of the ships

when you get lost, just orient yourself by the refinery
when you get turned around, look for the port
you can see the cranes from just about anywhere,

around here

AQUARIUM OF THE PACIFIC   *for Jonathan Skinner*

Too many ghosts reach out

                                             enjoy your flight

ghost of grass
ghost of poison
ghost of oil

                                             spill and seep

GREBE   blue footed dead one
ONCE
TWICE   by the curb in the gutter blue
                  [-miles/s from ocean]

GREAT BLUE HERON   great blue garbage
                                    feather heavy greatcoat
                                      singular eye

SEA OTTER   cyclist field notes
                      PCH in the gutter by
                      the curb [>1 mile from beach]
                      LAGUNA BEACH

Chihuahua   LONG BEACH soake to bloat
                      heavy storms
                      compose garden garbage
                      piles [20' from Pacific]

did I latch the windows each night
with such purpose
hours careen into longhand

to live among water
dust fluid to rise
small filament pops out burn glow gold

dim fuse

air heavy with roses plumeria night blooming jasmine datura wax jasmine

where you see language I see Sunday kayak side moon jelly

firm   "like a fish"

opal

lean

fresh float canal side between two vertical rifts concrete rebar

yacht (Alamitos Bay, LONG BEACH CALIFORNIA)

*

two sea nettles twist turn to backlit apricot blender
pale back light so two kale arms bob trail red venom ribbon tongues

but can't seem to get out from under urtica diocia's fine green prick
fully, to sea
                    [a landing]

*

Jake spied sea hares these aqua slugs ten times over again
slurp sea comb thick under water jelly

common least terns
wetland reclamation project
derricks
rot splinter wood grey glare

endangered sparrow
sea bottom
pipers plovers minnow minnow
fish

all in crustacean

gulls

pelican swam dive surface fishy neck'd

*

bivalves are elongate
BLACK TEGULA
dome shaped conical
cylindrical geometry of
shells
PACIFIC WHITE VENUS
CHANNELED DUCK CLAM
yoldia-shaped macoma
Inflated Pandora
shiny one thin dime

A BLEEDING TOOTH BI-VALVE
common American sundial

Chiton
Over
My
Most
Open
Neptune

A fine book most delicious travel tome emergency dilemma methods
ROUGH-GIRDLED CHITON igneous rock CHITON FUZZY in
deeper water important source of food mostly cold and temperate this
common cuttle bone

narrow ligament

deep depressions

CONTAINER ECONOMIES

```
HANJIN    EVERGREEN    COSCO
MAERSK SEA LAND TRITON APL
CONSOLIDATED FREIGHT LINES
BKO SANTA FE ROLLINS G.O.D.
HYUNDAI   CHINA   STAR   LINE
```

```
VINCENT   TERRAZANO   BRIDGE
700  SPRUNG  TONS  OF  LIT UP
TWISTEDSTEELSLUNGLOWWITH
PERFECT PITCH RUSTED TOOTH
JAW   KEEPS   EACH   SEAM  TIGHT
```

container
as the staple
vessel of modernity

FROM THE DEN OF SHIPS

were we servants to the nap
of our jeans

to the seduction of
cheap goods

sex

servants to the promise of portals

a better way

for whom

and by proxy of what

                              sicker old agent of change

for more or less soldier

dust burkha

*

SLEEP

was it enough to talk about politics
in our own home

to be unafraid at home

land of the free / home of the slaves

was our silent pretty face enough

our perfect hemmed-in-ness enough

to chant rhythms

behind teeth

our teeth of the night

*

in the den of ships we find I can't square the yacht with the mansion
hitched to the bank

flat water ocean

skimming the shore

can't square this ever sun with ever air
black sooty window sill
burnt rubber smell

Greetings from Beautiful Long Beach, California!

can't square our always thirst
poison water   chem-clean

one planet cargo
one planet hold

one moon refinery
one moon oil island

we don't intend to "live" here very long

anonymous "public"
Citizen Jane
oh empire
oh shipping
oh people fast asleep
we are the
what's hoped for
this
in the how now moment sullied biosphere
glacial ice the size of Connecticut—American
planetary measuring scale
shears off melting
science see it explode

CITIZEN JANE

ownership or loss
and "no bordered sense of that"
I do not know how we were to be (we) unbordered

there is always a border
your line in the sand
keep scratching—here—
let me move it here

cross over
tip
reach
berth
bunk
bunker
low-down
tether
nether
ships

language the blowhole
starts here
start stopping
heck of a dive and mast under
forewheel
every mizzen mild day
crow's nest to sea shore
cowrie shell commerce
conversations of necks
iron to jugular / such dead heavy load
bear down these century
while some pure poet's
pure reason
leaves the whole world

away

SECOND AQUARIUM FOR JONATHAN

this is the world we're making
low slung anaphora
burrows for mice

zebra mussel
sharp conduit science
cut brain path to seize

a bigger better bilge-water bomb
squat stow away Serbo-Croat
diaspora ship

cargo my Great Lakes
drink my Erie bitter swill
cutlass to foot soldier

push eyes on
young girls
pulling mussels

this world
one of conical sphere

this world
ellipsoid

tilting/tilt me
a lilting kind of love song goodbye

our speciest
garble speech
us fat pronoun
unmaking ourselves

come kitten
come polecat
come corvus
come ratty disaster aglow

we tramped through the night
thick misty all over
the narrow mountain path
scattered plastic to this world
of pallet wrap
Rubbermaid miasma

how this far from normal
how this close to piñon cedar
wrecked up dormant silver
mercury—mine

it followed us

it was too much to grasp

the mountain
once freeway
once cinder
once ash

FROM THE DEN OF SHIPS   (Two)

Catalogue of Earth Works

one lone serval free roams   *(January Hollywood Hills)*

Bengal tiger tracked to death   *(February Ventura County)*

waterbirds wash up dead oily   *(March Seal Beach)*

Great Blue Heron storm wrecked / wracked
fluffed feathers   a great blue great coat   dead awful   still standing

                                (Winter Storm Belmont Shore Beach)

dear Chihuahua (chee-hoo-uh-hoo-uh) washes up out to sea

                                                    and back again
                                (Winter Storm Long Beach)
flames of the port sky shot
                        orange cone
                            riot the sky
                                    daytime nighttime unending
(we three see this separate same time)

this goes on for days and days   *(Spring Long Beach)*

RULES OF THE PORT: Pacific engagement: Dislocate the facts: Report
SAN PEDRO: *Filipino community takes in sailors adrift*
TEN THOUSAND **COCKROACHES** FEAST ON NO FOOD *(NPR: 2/05)*

SPECIFIC ENGAGEMENT: Rain   dead **grebe**   dead **pelican**
dead **dog**   oil clog   ocean   soft **mollusk** gone sun side up

but could only see DYSTOPIA no perfect vision COUNTING
the dead no perfect vision no clear field no dream of a
BETTER bettor   what we inherit   what do we
OUR BROKEN our soil(ed) PURCHASE our
empty   endless   BLAH BLAH

POLITICS OF THE UNREAD

the directions maintain
fragments of "this"

pure pine pile up
sulfur rattlers bark

cut sharp with slant "L"
askance/the gaze/cut

to known pronoun/proverb/pro let aire
there is no other than that which already within you

but the bittern bark
the blades trace

path from ocean
sullied under coast

packed in like rats
shouldered up to one fine clatter manse

with no lawn

no nature

to speak of

*

but to maintain directions—
impropriety of no one

my child comes running
pier side/dry dock/ canal stink
lip
"sharks! big fish!"
and I too late for the glimpse

though having seen them too
the histories of fishes
blunt cut any path to narrative
or narrativity
voices/voiceless
swim

*

the way of it
the way

the place here
place of pronouns supple reach

place shark empty
place rays anchovy black jellies
pale listing to red tide

wetland reclamation space
they moved the highway

they built this island
they dredge the creamy
seamless
coast

to water to wetland to
piles to pinging depth charge
naval seal ship bevied
levied with fear
fear grips
who's the bigger dark lurker now?

*

these days
my materia medica
some bittern arsenal
some tern-like commission
to sneak in/pull yield

they're making nests for the killdeer
sapling white pelican lesser grebe
spoonbill skimmer sea hare
dainty mole crab
with her fine fiddler freight
orange roe cake
a sample for sale

response—an utterance
what words do rise up in iris
flipped gaze the mimic
to stutter arctic—or just tic

a long thigh a long thick
finger of grease
spill leak from something
these monstrous yachts
doth offend thee oh evermore
than any Ulsan oil seep

gutter to stillness
or smother the grunions
left offspring
eke out a living at the edge of such
opening gaps

layers of oil
one shiny magenta yellow blue
not distinct
indeterminate pure petrol
absolutely bad flow
fills my neighborhood

water artery wet streets
and us no boat to row—
so the watcher, come looker
what choice her
fine foot/tucks/sidewalk to city
beach
fine picking litter—the effronter
of dunderheaded gargantua
this bottle cap
condom
cup
and again

repeat into stillness

this weekend, next—what dates
what matter
again and again we do it

bend spines to the earth
our littoral zone

little oceans everywhere

economies of loss
cartographies of discontent

map our distance
a series of narrows / fully seamed gaps

lapse into—
long-distance reclamation projects

plumed distance / plumb depths
a new kind of dolphin depth charge

dropping a line
pulling up hosts / hostiles / a bigger anchor unwinds

coming up wet
down under

<ping>
<ping>

wait time
wait time

school of silent pupil fish
school of silent well paid them

*

intimate anachronist, intentional
root ganglia stop-gap
experiments of thought and dissolution
thinking processes
ground down tight
to the bone
dust

*

the slow ching-ching
pennies through finger

circadian pelican slip

do not eat WHITE CROAKER

toxin to wetland to needle to female
doggie plush tongue

**

I'm lacking the emotional
supra-engine

eering

lacking the necessary
emotional architecture

**

The Port of Los Angeles
emptied of all attachment
histories of colonies

life goes on here
it's raining
        quiet

—

polar sun iconic bear melt
bright blue bold hull

shoving out petrol: birth of the crude

hemmed in   liquid lancet
just in case   a spill

a boom a float a rubber—just in case
maybe holder catcher thing

impossible claws tooth metal
all in all / all and all to China
my P.R.C.

sweet skipper of every cheap rum
Target dresses

cents and cents and mattering
in the way of accumulation / discard

in the way of slow-towing petroleum coke down the coast (to MEXICO)
can you feel the tether thicken

capital umbilicus
bunched wisdom

a sea lion followed us out
reflected on purpose

pushed the white off the page

FUCK YOUR PASTORAL

in summer, we return
return to horses
we are horses
we are the flat hand
a horse licking pancake
a chicken eats sand
we are the chicken
and the sand

the grit of necessary

we are the bound coop
its dirtied edge also—
we are all these things at the same time

                                              as inside

the city   creeps

we are the soiled heron
the oiled grebes
we are every water bird
                    night flier
                    and also

the eye of the grebe the blue of
its foot
we are the crack of the terns
Bolsa Chica   all over
                    it's in us

but still

                more so

we are the flat hand
the horse tongue
that softness   that wet

we are the stick of oat to molasses
we are also
                    at the same time
the soot
we are also   at the same time
the worker
                    tearing down the façade
                    sandblasting signage
                    "MEATS DRY GOODS
                    PROVISIONS"

we are the winding tracks
                    the trainyard
and also the lip of the worker
blowing his smoke her smoke   us   ours
ten minutes
til mix up cement

we are the tenant   (come lovely
                    come high heel
                    come suit—)

we are the pen
inking the lease

we are the blue black ink spreading

spreading the making
                    all over

in summer, we go 'home'

but what is home

what is home

a question

we go back 'there'

        back east

go forward

            but it's back

we go home

watch frogs

in the storm drain

we watch it dry from wet to mud to cracking dirt to dust to—
nothing

nothing but a drain ditch   once more

all frogs   all gone

we watch swallows we keep
calling them "sparrows" (and keep
getting it wrong) this is the
sparrow our city our backyard bird
(home) inside us

inside the mind of
the thinking

of us

we go home in "wellness"

we go our bags packed

stacked flying open

we go together   and apart

we go

we return

we go again

we return

we grow more and more confused

which home of us

which is this

we spin

first this way

then that way

we want to fix a place on

the map

but we can't help the feel

wake up in the garden

both sides both flowered

we keep waking

and being blossoms nodding

head folded sepal dropping

petal slim nectar whisked out

as we are also

slim tongue

softer sphinx moth

louder humming   bird

and the brook and the thistle

the elder   berry

we keep being all these things

at the same time

it is too much knowing of

watching

it is too much fast

too much softly

it is too much as the neck

of a horse is too much

as the ship of us backyard

too much

as the delicate of mine too much

as too much of mine.

too much of wanting

it is all too much.

even as

haying the field

as the gasoline's tractor

as the snakes runneth over

as vultures come pick

even as frighten the goslings

the gander angers the man

even as the man brick-gentle

brick-gentle as man

as we puzzle

we puzzle and fix

we women we apron we working

we apron working too much

we children we digging

we digging too much

we digging we stacking up

soldiers their plastic green

their soldier plastic dusting

as over there some other

their soldier plastic dusting

moves over muscle

but here

we digging

we haying

we watching the sky

we fire rockets

build a very tiny submarine

we together

we all this together now

breaking apart

we all breaking

we all breaking we all

as we are not (all)

as we are not this (we)

moving backward to the place of relations broken and sold
moving back to the place of my belongings uprooted
back to all my alive there and with me
back to the place of all my relations sound in body in mind
back to the place of the living and the dead
to walk among me now

I was this thing
thing fitting together
and the aperture opening close
I was the retrofit gleam in its eye
wave under foremast
and the knuckle at wheel
I was all these things at the same time
moving forward backward still

I movement had no such pace
I movement had no such lifting of rhythms
as my argument passed through my teeth
as my argument entered I ear
as my counter gaze glanced backward
I glance moving forward moving backward again
repeat into stillness

I was all these things

I was the hand of the child placing the ink and this child was also me
and my child and there was no ownership between us

I was regarding myself the hand of the child placing the ink drawing
pictures on skin I was his skin and her skin I was also the image fixed there
and looking

blink of the spider
turn of the dolphin
chip of the steel
spin of the turnstile
I was the gelatin holding it close
holding my image to myself I was all these things at the same time

and none of it at all.

I was a dream of myself or was I
righting the wrong
severing slowly
singing to myself

sing herons ungreasy
sing ships move backwards slowly
sing oil skim off water
sing oil skim off the grebes
sing sea otters breath back into

singing mucus from lungs

sing derricks to rusting
sing gears into freeze

I was singing with a closed mouth

singing thinking

sing no more anger between me
sing no more stillness no breakwater

sing come away slowly
sing carry me home

to no home

sing sound of the breath in my ocean
sing I am the ocean between
sing make and unmake
disorder
sing lithium sweet breeze
sing balm
sing cool cloth to your forehead my forehead sing quiet down visions
sing now raise up
sing now raise up
sing now raise up bones
sing now knitting
sing now delicate grass
sing now softer

this was my voice
this was my wind
my hover
my spitting the sound
my slow now
my leave us
my sleeping

my bookend
my bounty
my overload hull

my cranes of metal and wing
my atoms fixing to listen

my black jellies
my red tide
my anchovy phosphorescing
my reach

my withdraw

I was all this and running

still I was running the turbine backwards to flow
I was running the carbine the platelets
I was running the cooler from empty to stocked to full to feeding the crew
the sailors set drifting I was undoing the cramp in their belly I was undoing
the cockroaches feast undoing the open undoing the beds the bunks the
landed and wet I was undoing

all this as I was unchocking missles snug in their holds

undoing the hands of the volunteers I was unvolunteering
undoing the reading the learn
undoing the language
undoing shame grief hunger

I was undoing all this as I undid the spool
the radio's wheel
unmagnetizing tape
unzipping the case
I emptying notebook erasing the names
unwriting the manifest
unnaming the ship

I unforging metal
unriveting plates
I unbruising the shoulder
I withdrawing the balm

I became unnecessary

I became without myself

I became a column holding up cedar

a column holding up marble

I became a pre-fabricated steel I-beam

I became soft as metal to melting

I became melting

I became ore restored to the earth

I became the spine of seventeen small children

I spine of children curled into darkness

I became the rope lifting slowly

rope hitched to their waist

I became the selling undoing

selling of seventeen Untouchable children girl children
holding up marble

I became myself backwards became them
I became them unmarbled became them unowned

I was doing all this while I down in I valley off of I-88
I became rasp of the cock's crow
I became the rooster Colonel again
before the lead bullet

before chasing with spangles before the sharp of his spur

I became the spur too

and the spur in our hearts

our hearts set against him

became his feathers

and wind under I wing

and the soot in the wing in the wind sifting to water

slow drip of asbestos

slow drip of tamoxifen

slow drip of the cave

stalactite soda straw angel wing slab bacon cave popcorn

I became all these things at the same time

knit of the thistle

span between finger

wing web between thumb

line of the palmist

line of iris

line of lenscap

line of time flipping backward

twisting to breech

I became dust and soot and the sticky of coxcomb honey mud milk

I became

I was

I therefore

and so too

I also

I anyhow

I loved

I slept

I was

and am still

all

but before I lay down to nest in

before I settled and doze

I took mine hand mine others

I took them I folded

I tucked the shirt to the belly to the child to bedsheet to window to water

to glow

I caressed

I caressed backward and slowly

undid all the doing

unwrote my name inky

unwrote mine page

unkissed

unlifted my toe step

my tiptoe

my foothold

my webbing

wing

hustle

chat

I lifted these from places I'd marked in

and people

unpeopled heart broken

unlistened heart secret

undid

and then

unopened the port

unopened breakwater

I opened

I breathed

I was

I

I

I

eye aye

ai

eh

eh now

oh dear

oh comeaway

oh comeaway

oh come

oh ocean

oh crevice

caressing

oh I oh only

oh now

oh

oh

oh I'm

I'm oh

I only

I alone

I always

I every

I all

but still—
I was not done with we
I had more to do
more work
more travel
more touching I hands
more touching doorknob subway rail
more touching transmission
more wing web wheel
more I lettered and named

colored in

still questions flew up in I
noticing too

how we I
became strange to one another
became container ships moving into and out of the same ports
the same ports all over

we became directed and flowed
became our bilge water and ballast also
we became the containers
tipped stacked together commiserate
containing, contained
so many ships together
utterly separate

we became in the mouths of
became perpetuated
on MTV NGC LEGO
we became all over

were we we or were we
containers contained
moving

mingling and all within our each
our metal porous borders
remembering almost nothing of what we told ourselves
whether we were Los Angeles Seoul New Orleans Beijing
whether we agreed or did not agree with the expansiveness of our we
flexing certain torque
whether we agreed or did not agree we were electric bodies fitting space

there was a same thirst
a same want of the lungs to fill
and cleanly
a same want of smaller spaces
among us to be touched
more or less lovingly
with more or less friction

whether we wanted this or not

it was there

was us

defining us we

all the time now.

we became strange to ourselves

and each other

stranger

desiring knowing and being known

desiring this all the time now

moving us as we did   CASPIAN
                                  PACIFIC
                                  ATLANTIC
                                  BLACK
                                  GULF

we mixed

and became more so

but also singular—mixing singular

alone

About the Author

Jane Sprague's poems, reviews and essays have been published in various print and online journals including *Xcp: Cross-Cultural Poetics, How2, Jacket, Tinfish, ecopoetics, Primary Writing, Tarpaulin Sky* and others. Her chapbooks include *break / fast, monster: a bestiary, Entropic Liberties* (with Jonathan Skinner), *Sacking the Henwife* and *Apache Roadkill,* among others. Recent publications include the book *Belladonna* Elders Series No. 8* with poets Tina Darragh and Diane Ward. She teaches at Cal State Long Beach and the Workshop for Language and Thinking at Bard College. She edits and publishes Palm Press in Long Beach, California, where she lives with her family.

Chax Press is located in the Tucson Historic Warehouse Arts District, in the Small Planet Bakery Building. Please contact us at *chax@theriver.com*, and visit our web site at *http://chax.org*, where you will also find the chax-blog. In 2009 we celebrate our 25th birthday with the year-long project *A Leap Is Now!* of which this book is part. Chax Press receives support from the Tucson Pima Arts Council, and from the Arizona Commission on the Arts, with funding from the State of Arizona and the National Endowment for the Arts. We depend on donations from readers like you, and you may give to Chax Press on our web site, or contact us for more information. Here are some of our recent titles; many more are found on our web site.

Joel Bettridge, *Presocratic Blues*
Linh Dinh, *Some Kind of Cheese Orgy*
Jonathan Rothschild, *The Last Clubhouse Eulogy*
Jacque Vaught Brogan, *ta(l)king eyes*
Jeanne Heuving, *Transducer*
John Tritica, *Sound Remains*
Patrick Pritchett, *Salt, My Love: A Ballad* (letterpress book arts)
Kathleen Fraser and Nancy Tokar Miller, *Witness* (letterpress book arts)
CA Conrad, *The Book of Frank*
Michael Cross, *In Felt Treeling*
Steve McCaffery, *Slightly Left of Thinking*
Karen Mac Cormack, *Implexures* (complete edition)